Reggie Rat

Seven Short Bedtime Stories

Book Three

First published in the UK by Finshoo Publishing 2024

The right of Finshoo Publishing and Craig Ansell to be identified as the author of this work has been asserted by them in accordance with the Copyright, Designs and Patents Act 1988, all rights reserved.

Text © Craig Ansell 2024
Illustrations © Janette Hill 2024

ISBN 978 1 7395792 2 7

All rights reserved.

This book is a work of fiction, characters, places, names, adventures and dialogues are all products of the author's imagination or are used fictitiously. Any resemblance to actual people, events or locales is entirely coincidental.

This book is sold subject to the condition that it shall not, by way of trade, be hired, lent out or otherwise circulated in any form of binding or cover than that in which it is published. No part of this publication may be reproduced, stored in a retrieval system, or transmitted in any form or by any other means without the prior permission of Finshoo Publishing.

This book is dedicated to my son

Charlie

for being the most caring and ambitious man
a proud father could wish for.

Good evening, readers and listeners

These adorable short bedtime stories of Reggie Rat and all his faithful friends have been in our family for four generations, until now, that is.

Our family have enjoyed these tales of adventure for so long that I now want to share them with you, so that you and your family can enjoy these stories as much as we did and still do today.

Sweet dreams...

Craig Ansell

Introduction

These seven adorable, exciting, courageous, and entertaining short bedtime stories are full of adventure with a Rat called Reggie and his faithful friends.

Reggie Rat lives in a very, very clean sewer near the ancient hills of Rough Hill Woods. Reggie Rat has many friends; each character is as inspiring and captivating as the other. There's Bertie Badger, his very, very bestest friend, Vinnie Vole, Harry Hare, and many more.

Whether you're the listener or reader, Reggie Rat welcomes you into his family of friends, where you too can hang out, play, learn and have fun.

So, join in and let your imagination run away with these fantastic tales of adventure…

Contents

Monday Night
Reggie Rat and the Magic Tree

Tuesday Night
Reggie Rat gets a New Bike

Wednesday Night
Reggie Rat Visits a Medieval Moat House

Thursday Night
Reggie Rat goes to the Theatre

Friday Night
Reggie Rat and the Rainbow

Saturday Night
Reggie Rat goes on Holiday

Sunday Night
Reggie Rat at the Seaside

Monday Night
Reggie Rat and the Magic Tree

Today was the day Reggie Rat and all his friends agreed to meet at the bottom of the hill in Rough Hill Woods before heading to the top to play at the Magic Tree; it's not really a Magic Tree; this is just what they call it.

This is where all the friends hang out and enjoy spending time together. Last summer, they made a swing out of an old rope and a tyre and hung it from the Magic Tree.

Bertie Badger was the first one there, pushing through the bushes and twitching his long black and white snout.

He was followed by Dani Dormouse, searching her way through the bramble bushes with her big black, round eyes while sniffing the air with her pink nose and long whiskers.

Then, Harry Hare ran up the lane with his big, strong back legs and long, floppy ears.

Vinnie Vole was next, who seemed to take her time sniffing the air with her little nose and short whiskers. Finally, Reggie Rat and Rebecca Rabbit made their way there together, holding hands.

"*Come on, let's go and play on the swing!*" shouted Harry Hare.

"*Okay, I'll race you there!*" shouted Rebecca Rabbit.

So, off they all went, running as fast as they could.

The first one to the top was Harry Hare, then Rebecca Rabbit, then Reggie Rat, followed by Vinnie Vole and Dani Dormouse.

> Reggie Rat wants to know, do you know who was the last one to reach the Magic Tree?

> Well, it was Bertie Badger, of course, puffing and panting.

Bertie Badger was a little unhappy and a little upset for being the last one to reach the top.

"*Don't worry,*" said Reggie Rat, trying to cheer him up, "*We can't all be good at everything we do.*"

"*That's right, it's about taking part and having fun; that's what matters,*" said Rebecca Rabbit, giving Bertie Badger a big hug.

"*Thank you, you are all so kind; from now on, I will never be upset for being the last one,*" Bertie Badger replied, feeling much better.

Because Harry Hare arrived first, he jumped straight onto the tyre swing.

"Push me, push me, please, someone push me!" he shouted.

Bertie Badger was the only one big enough and strong enough to push him.

"*See, you're the strongest one here and the only one who can push Harry Hare out of all of us,*" encouraged Reggie Rat.

Bertie Badger puffed out his chest and gave one almighty push, followed by another, then another, again and again he went.

"*Not so hard, Bertie Badger, I might get tangled up in all the branches!*" shouted Harry Hare.

But, being in a silly mood, Bertie Badger did not take any notice and kept pushing as hard as possible.

Everyone shouted at Bertie Badger, "*Slow down, slow down!*"

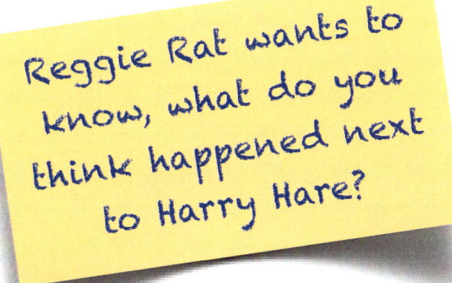

Reggie Rat wants to know, what do you think happened next to Harry Hare?

Well, Harry Hare got stuck in the branches of the Magic Tree of course.

"*Oh no, I'm very, very sorry; I'll get you down as quickly as I can,*" said Bertie Badger, wondering what he should do.

"*I told you this would happen!*" shouted Harry Hare, "*Get me down, get me down!*"

"*Harry Hare, you must be brave; you will be okay,*" assured Dani Dormouse, "*Reggie Rat will think of a way to get you down.*"

"*Well, we could shake the tree until he falls out,*" suggested Bertie Badger, grabbing the tree.

"*No, no, stop; I don't think that's a good idea; he might fall and hurt himself,*" replied Vinnie Vole.

"*Got it!*" yelled Reggie Rat, "*I need someone fast on their feet to go and ask Mr Bull in the big field at the bottom of the hill to help us.*"

"*I'll go; I'm the second fastest here!*" replied Rebecca Rabbit.

So, off she went, running as fast as she could, jumping over tree stumps in and out of bushes until finally, she made it to the big field at the bottom of the hill.

"*Help, help!*" shouted Rebecca Rabbit, looking for Mr Bull.

"*Calm down, calm down,*" said Mr Bull, as he grazed on some grass, "*What seems to be the problem?*"

"*It's my friend Harry Hare; he's stuck up our Magic Tree, and we can't get him down!*" shouted Rebecca Rabbit, still trying to catch her breath.

Reggie Rat wants to know, do you know how big a bull can grow?

Well, a bull can grow to 6 feet tall and 7 feet long.

"*Of course, I can help,*" replied Mr Bull, "*You mentioned a Magic Tree; well, come on then, let's get going.*"

Mr Bull plodded along, and Rebecca Rabbit tried to hurry him along to help Harry Hare escape from the Magic Tree.

Everyone was very, very happy to see Mr Bull, who began to help lower Harry Hare down from the Magic Tree.

He was soon safe with his feet firmly back on the ground; his friend Bertie Badger was the first to hug him.

"*I'm very, very sorry,*" said a relieved Bertie Badger, squeezing Harry Hare a little harder.

Everyone clapped, cheered and thanked Mr Bull for helping before he plodded off to his big field at the bottom of the hill.

After they had finished hanging out together, they talked and laughed about how Harry Hare got stuck up the Magic Tree and all because sometimes badgers can be slightly silly at times.

Sweet dreams from Reggie Rat

Tuesday Night
Reggie Rat gets a New Bike

Reggie Rat was on his way to the bike shop with his dad, where he was to pick up his brand-new mountain bike.

Luckily, reaching the bike shop took little time, as he was super excited.

"*Here we are; come on, Dad, Mr Fox will be waiting for us!*" yelled Reggie Rat excitedly.

Mr Fox has owned the bike shop for many years; his father used to own the shop before him. Mr Fox has the most remarkable shiny orangey-red silk coat and wears a brown apron with a large pocket at the front to hold all his tools when working.

Into the shop ran Reggie Rat as fast as he could, tripping up over the doorstep right into the arms of Mr Fox.

"Steady as you go, master Reggie Rat," greeted Mr Fox with a big smile as he caught Reggie Rat from landing on the floor.

"Good catch, Mr Fox, have you got it, have you, have you got it!" shouted Reggie Rat eagerly.

"Yes, of course, it's out the back; wait here, and I'll go and fetch it," replied Mr Fox.

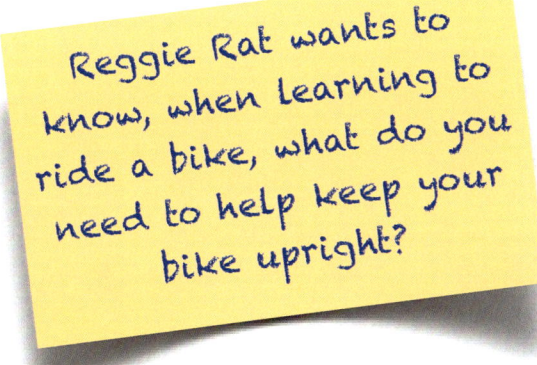

Reggie Rat wants to know, when learning to ride a bike, what do you need to help keep your bike upright?

Well, you will need some stabilisers to help keep your bike upright.

After a few minutes, Mr Fox returned with a cool, bright yellow mountain bike with 18 gears and big wide wheels for off-roading.

"Wow, will you just look at that? That's the best bike I ever saw!" smiled Reggie Rat. *"I can't wait to show this to my friend Bertie Badger."*

Mr Fox explained how all the parts worked while Reggie Rat listened and asked questions to understand how to operate his new shiny, bright yellow mountain bike.

"The bike has had a service, and it's ready to go; all the gears are set up, so you shouldn't have any problems," informed Mr Fox.

"Thank you for all your hard work, Mr Fox," replied Reggie Rat.

Mr Rat looked at Reggie Rat and smiled; he was so proud that he took the time to thank Mr Fox for all his hard work.

Reggie Rat wants to know, what should he wear on his head to keep himself safe while riding his bike?

Well, he should wear a helmet on his head of course.

"Have you got a selection of helmets?" asked Mr Rat.

"Yes, over there; feel free to try them on," replied Mr Fox.

Looking at all the helmets, Reggie Rat soon spotted one that he liked the look of. He pulled the matching bright yellow helmet from the shelf, plopped it onto his head, and fastened the buckle.

Reggie Rat wants to know, what should he have on his bike so he can be seen clearly?

Well, he should have some lights on his bike of course.

"Remember, it's not good to ride your bike in the dark, but having lights switched on in the daytime also means you can be seen by others much better," informed Mr Fox.

"I understand, Dad. Please, can I have some lights, too?" asked Reggie Rat, *"These lights are cool; what do you think?"*

"Yes, of course, Mr Fox does have an excellent point; they will do, and I like the helmet you have chosen too," replied Mr Rat.

Reggie Rat looked his new bright yellow mountain bike up and down and noticed something strange in his wheel spokes.

"They are called reflectors; they also help you to be seen in the dark," explained Mr Fox, *"So be sure not to take them off."*

"Well, I believe we are all done here, thank you, Mr Fox; we will have the helmet, and I'll take these lights, too," said Mr Rat, getting out his wallet to pay Mr Fox.

"Goodbye, Mr Fox and thank you again," waved Reggie Rat.

Once the bike was securely placed into the car, they started the short journey back to Rough Hill Woods.

Suddenly, Reggie Rat had a great idea as they approached the edge of Rough Hill Woods.

"Dad, would you be so kind as to drop me off here so I can ride the rest of the way home?" asked Reggie Rat.

So, out came the mountain bike and on went his safety gear.

"I'll race you home, Dad!" shouted Reggie Rat, riding off and ringing his bell.

"*Slow down, it's not a race,*" yelled Mr Rat.

But he never heard his dad and carried on, weaving in and out of bushes and jumping over fallen trees.

Mr Rat stood there and watched him ride off into the distance, mud flicking up from behind his back wheel.

"*Yahoo!*" yelled Reggie Rat, peddling as fast as he could.

Changing gears just as Mr Fox had shown him, he darted in and out of the trees, up and down the hills and along the paths.

As he approached home, he saw his dad was almost there, so he changed gear and peddled harder to try and beat him.

It wasn't long before he made it; he had the biggest smile and looked like he had the best time riding his new but now dirty yellow mountain bike through Rough Hill Woods.

Reggie Rat skidded to a stop outside his front door; he jumped off his bike and stood there admiring it.

He noticed his dad pulling up, so he jumped back on his dirty yellow mountain bike and peddled towards him, ringing the bell and making Mrs Rat come out to see what was happening.

"*That's a lovely-looking bike,*" smiled Mrs Rat, "*Although it would appear it needs a good clean.*"

"*Thank you, Mum, and thank you, Dad, for my mountain bike; I've just had the best time ever,*" replied a happy Reggie Rat.

Sweet dreams from Reggie Rat

Wednesday Night
Reggie Rat Visits a Medieval Moat House

Mr & Mrs Rat have the day off work and wanted to do something interesting and exciting.

Mrs Rat had suggested going to the medieval moat house, which stood over the hills but wasn't too far away.

"That is a great idea," said Mr Rat, and asked if Reggie Rat would like to bring a friend.

"Can I, can I? That's awesome!" thanked Reggie Rat excitedly.

Reggie Rat sat down and contemplated who he should invite.

"I'm going to ask Bobby Black Bird, my new friend from school," said Reggie Rat, *"That way, I can get to know him better."*

"That's a lovely idea," replied Mrs Rat, smiling.

Well, it wasn't long before everyone was ready, and they were all on their way to the medieval moat house.

As they got nearer, Reggie Rat could see the top of the roof peering through the lush green treetops that swayed to and from.

"We're here, we're here!" yelled Reggie Rat.

"Calm down," said Mr Rat, sneezing into his handkerchief.

> Reggie Rat wants to know, do you know what's special about a medieval moat house?

> Well, there is a moat, that is full of water that surrounds the house with only a small bridge that leads to the main door.

Wiping his nose, Mr Rat drove down a long gravel driveway, following the signs directing him to the car park.

On their way, they could see many beautiful trees; Mr Rat knew the names of the trees and pointed them out to Reggie Rat and Bobby Black Bird.

"That is a big gigantic oak tree; that one is a silver birch, and over there is a sweet chestnut," informed Mr Rat.

That got Reggie Rat thinking, *"I wonder what type of tree our Magic Tree is at the top of the hill back in Rough Hill Woods."*

Mr Rat pulled into the car park, parked up, and they all got out.

The medieval moat house looked very, very imposing, with its rugged tiled roof, hand-carved brickwork, and brightly coloured lead windows.

As they began to walk towards the medieval moat house, they could see the old stone bridge that took them across the moat to the main door.

The grand main door was made from an oak tree seeded over seven hundred years ago; it has a very, very large brass door knocker in the shape of a lion's head.

"I've got a great idea!" said Bobby Black Bird, *"I'm going to fly around and see the medieval moat house from high up in the sky."*

"That's a great idea," replied Reggie Rat.

So, off flew Bobby Black Bird, flapping his feathery black wings as hard and fast as possible.

Before you knew it, Bobby Black Bird looked very, very small, way up in the sky.

Whilst flying around and around, Bobby Black Bird glided over the moat that was full of water.

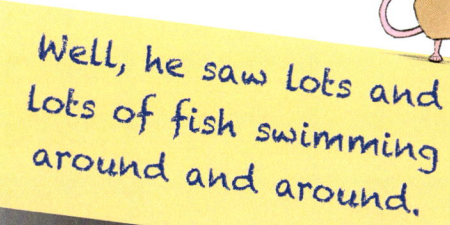

Reggie Rat wants to know, can you guess what Bobby Black Bird saw swimming around in the water?

Well, he saw lots and lots of fish swimming around and around.

"I can see everything from up here, including the fish in the moat," screamed Bobby Black Bird towards Reggie Rat.

Mr & Mrs Rat followed Reggie Rat as he went over the bridge through the gatehouse and entered the courtyard.

"So many flowers and all different colours," smiled Reggie Rat, smelling some roses in the courtyard.

Bobby Black Bird's wings started getting tired, so he thought now was a good time to fly back to his friend.

"You looked like you were having so much fun flying around and around," said Reggie Rat, smiling.

"I did, but I wish I were strong enough to fly with you on my back," replied Bobby Black Bird, "We could have enjoyed the views together."

"It's okay, but thank you for considering me," replied Reggie Rat, "Come on, let's go and see the grand dining room and library!"

They entered the medieval moat house and went to the grand dining room, where they saw many paintings on the walls.

"These paintings are the portraits of all the Lords and Ladies who lived here right back through history," said a voice from behind a grand piano, *"Hello, I'm Mr Goat. I'm a volunteer here and will happily answer any questions."*

Without hesitation, *"How many fish do you have in the moat?"* asked Bobby Black Bird, *"There were too many for me to count."*

Reggie Rat thought this was a funny question to ask and giggled.

"Hmm, I don't know the answer to that question," replied Mr Goat, looking slightly puzzled.

"I've got one," said Reggie Rat, *"When was this medieval moat house built?"*

"Good question, in 1484 by Lord Benedict Black Bird," replied Mr Goat, pointing to his portrait on the wall above the fireplace.

Reggie Rat looked at Bobby Black Bird and said, *"Hey, you could be an ancestor of the late Lord Benedict Black Bird."*

"I could, I could," replied Bobby Black Bird, puffing out his chest.

"That was a funny question about the fish," giggled Reggie Rat, *"I think we're going to become great friends."*

After more exploring and reading about all the interesting facts, it was soon time for everyone to go home.

Sweet dreams from Reggie Rat

Thursday Night
Reggie Rat goes to the Theatre

Reggie Rat and all his friends had planned to visit the Big Mound Theatre near Rough Hill Woods. 'The Adventures of Wendy and Peter Pan' was being performed, they didn't want to miss this.

Reggie Rat had made his way to the theatre with his friends Bertie Badger and Harry Hare.

While they walked along the path, they stopped to see who could do the most press-ups.

Bertie Badger could do the most press-ups between the three, as he loved to keep his muscles looking strong.

Whenever they do their press-ups, they always encourage each other; this helps them squeeze out a few more reps.

Soon, they arrived at the Big Mound Theatre, where they all went and washed their hands after getting dirty doing those press-ups.

'This way," pointed Reggie Rat towards the theatre doors.

As they got closer, they had to queue patiently before entering through the enormous golden doors. Once through, they found themselves in a rather wonderful theatre setting.

They could see many bright stage lights shining in the distance, lighting the stage in different colours.

When they finally arrived at the front of the queue, a helpful usher guided them with her torch and showed them their seats.

They thanked the usher for being helpful and sat down, ready for the show to begin.

Reggie Rat wants to know, can you guess who else came to the theatre?

Well, it was Rebecca Rabbit, Dani Dormouse and Vinnie Vole.

Looking down towards the stage, they all imagined what it would be like if they were to perform in a play.

Rebecca Rabbit, Dani Dormouse and Vinnie Vole were also shown to their seats that just so happened to be right behind the boys; they all had some of the best seats in the theatre.

"*Howdy, boys!*" they all said together as they sat down and made themselves comfortable.

"*Are we all looking forward to seeing the show?*" whispered Dani Dormouse, licking some ice cream.

"*Yes, yes, yes,*" the boys replied.

They were all very, very excited to see the show as they hadn't seen this performance before.

All eyes peered down towards the theatre stage, where they could make out that four elegantly decorated beds were right in the middle of the stage, each highlighted with a spotlight.

Suddenly, "*Shussssh*" could be heard from the audience across the theatre.

Dressed in pyjamas, Wendy and her three brothers danced onto the stage.

It wasn't long before Peter Pan entered the stage, flying through the air and whisking Wendy off to Neverland.

Reggie Rat and all his friends were mesmerised while watching the show.

Smoking dry ice spread through the audience, music surrounded the theatre in all directions, and dramatic acrobats flew through the air, delighting all with imagination and adventure.

Suddenly, the music became dramatically louder and louder, creating the most incredible atmosphere within the theatre.

This was because the nasty Captain Hook came onto the stage.

Captain Hook had a giant ship called the Jolly Roger, and he was the arch-enemy of Peter Pan; his pirate crew on board the Jolly Roger were always fighting with Peter Pan.

Reggie Rat wants to know, can you guess why he was called Captain Hook?

Well, Captain Hook had a hook instead of his hand because he got into a terrible fight with a crocodile.

During the show, there were many sword fights between Captain Hook and Peter Pan.

But, during the last sword fight, Captain Hook fell from his ship into the water, the same water where the fierce crocodile swam; he had already bitten Captain Cook's hand off during their last encounter.

Snap, snap went the fierce crocodile as Captain Hook fought back, but this time, he finally lost against the crocodile, and big cheers roared across the theatre when Captain Hook finally met his match.

The audience then clapped with applause as the show ended.

"That was the best show I've ever seen; I liked how Captain Hook met his match with the crocodile," said Vinnie Vole.

"I, too, liked the ending," replied Harry Hare, re-enacting the sword fight scene with Bertie Badger.

As they all left the theatre, they were all very, very happy, so happy they pretended to be pirates all the way home.

Sweet dreams from Reggie Rat

Friday Night
Reggie Rat and the Rainbow

Rain was pouring down over Rough Hill Woods; everything was getting very, very wet, but this did not matter because Reggie Rat was inside, keeping dry and warm.

Sitting by the window, he would watch the rain pouring down while completing the homework given to him by his teacher.

As the rain began to stop, Reggie Rat could see all the woodland creatures leave their homes to enjoy the sunshine and drink the fresh rainwater left on the leaves of the surrounding trees.

Harry Hare was jumping up and down outside his window, trying to get his attention from in the garden; Reggie Rat wondered why Harry Hare was so excited.

"Have you seen the rainbow?" asked Harry Hare excitedly, pointing to the most magnificent rainbow you will ever see.

"Wow, will you just look at that!" replied Reggie Rat, looking up towards the sky.

"Shall we go and try to find the end of the rainbow?" asked Harry Hare, eager to get going.

"What a great idea!" replied Reggie Rat, *"I'll be right down."*

It hadn't been long before they were on their way when they lost sight of the rainbow and didn't know which way to go.

"Let's go to the Magic Tree," suggested Reggie Rat," *We should be able to see the rainbow from on top of the hill."*

They ran as fast as they could, Reggie Rat doing his best to keep up with Harry Hare.

"Come on, Reggie Rat, we are almost there!" shouted Harry Hare.

When they got to the Magic Tree, there was a tiny opening in the woods at the top of the hill; this gave them another glimpse of the rainbow.

> Reggie Rat wants to know, do you know the saying that helps you remember the colours of the rainbow?

> Well, the old saying that his grandad taught him is 'Richard Of York Gave Battle In Vain'. There's seven colours in total, Red, Orange, Yellow, Green, Blue, Indigo, Violet.

Now they could see the way; there was no time to waste, so they ran off as fast as they could.

Suddenly, a shadow covered them, followed by a deep voice.

"This way, if you are trying to get to the rainbow's end," said a big dark buzzard, swooping down.

Turning direction, Reggie Rat and Harry Hare began to follow the buzzard's enormous, dark, shadowy wings.

"Keep following my shadow," bellowed the big dark buzzard, *"We don't have much time."*

"What do you mean?" asked Harry Hare.

"The rainbow only lasts briefly," replied Reggie Rat.

The big dark buzzard continued to bellow, *"The legend has it that there is a pot of gold at the rainbow's end; although an Irish Leprechaun guards the pot of gold, but I'm sure he will share some of it with us."*

"A pot of gold!" screamed Harry Hare, looking at Reggie Rat.

"*An Irish Leprechaun!*" shouted Reggie Rat, looking at Harry Hare.

They could tell they were all getting closer as the rainbow was getting bigger and bigger.

> Reggie Rat wants to know, do you know what colour clothes an Irish Leprechaun wears?

> Well, an Irish Leprechaun wears green clothes with an Irish cap.

Jumping over fallen trees, diving through bushes and ducking under branches, they ran as fast as they could.

"*I'm Benjamin Buzzard, by the way; pleased to meet you,*" roared Benjamin Buzzard as he swooped up and down.

"*I'm Reggie Rat, and this is my friend, Harry Hare,*" shouted Reggie Rat back to him.

"*Quick this way,*" Benjamin Buzzard roared again.

Running out into the open, the rainbow looked so beautiful, with all seven colours as bright as the other; it looked magical.

Benjamin Buzzard was so excited that he started doing loop de loops high in the sky before swooping down.

Then, just like that, the rainbow started to fade, the colours dimming in the bright blue sky.

"*No, no!*" screamed Harry Hare, suddenly coming to a stop.

Reggie Rat skidded to a stop next to Harry Hare, looked up and noticed the rainbow had gone completely.

"Never mind, there is always next time," bellowed Benjamin Buzzard as he flew away.

"We'll get it next time," shouted Reggie Rat, waving him goodbye.

"Yes, next time," yelled Harry Hare, waving goodbye.

Sweet dreams from Reggie Rat

Saturday Night
Reggie Rat goes on Holiday

It was a beautiful summer morning in Rough Hill Woods; the sky was bright blue with scattered white fluffy clouds for as far as the eye could see.

Reggie Rat had woken up in the best mood because today was the start of his holiday.

Every year since Reggie Rat was a baby, Mr & Mrs Rat have always had a holiday by the seaside.

Reggie Rat wants to know, can you guess what he likes to build when he's on the beach?

Well, Reggie Rat likes to build sand castles of course.

This year, his very, very bestest friend Bertie Badger would also be coming along to share the adventures.

This excited Reggie Rat so much that he waited by the window, looking for Bertie Badger to turn up, as it wouldn't be long before Mr & Mrs Badger dropped him off.

One minute went by, then five minutes, then ten minutes.

"*Oooh, where is Bertie Badger!*" shouted Reggie Rat.

Well, the shouting got his mum's attention.

"*Reggie Rat! Patience is a virtue; Bertie Badger will be here soon enough,*" said Mrs Rat in a fair but firm voice, "*So, please stop shouting; it really is unnecessary.*"

"*Sorry, Mum, it's just that I'm so excited to be going on holiday with my friend, but I don't understand why he's not here yet,*" replied a sad-looking Reggie Rat.

Honk, honk went the sound of a car pulling up outside.

"*Looks like they have just turned up, a little late, but not to worry,*" said Mr Rat, "*Let's get the car packed, and we'll soon be on our way for some sun, fun and adventure.*"

Reggie Rat wants to know, what should he pack in his bag, that he can put on his feet, when he goes to the beach while on holiday?

Well, he should pack his flip-flops of course.

Knock, knock, knock went the door knocker.

"*I'll get it,*" yelled Reggie Rat, skidding round the corner and racing to open the door.

"*Hello everyone, so sorry for being late. Only we ran into some trouble with a flat tyre!*" explained Mr Badger.

Reggie Rat ran straight out the door and over to Bertie Badger, where they high-fived each other.

"Let's get your bags!" yelled Reggie Rat.

"Okeydokey," Bertie Badger replied as he told Reggie Rat about their flat tyre.

Once the car was packed, the boot firmly shut, and everyone was ready to go, Mr & Mrs Badger called to Bertie Badger.

"Be good and watch your manners for Mr & Mrs Rat," said Mr Badger, peering over his glasses perched on his long snout.

"I will, I will," replied Bertie Badger, standing to attention.

"That's good, and remember we love you very, very dearly," smiled Mrs Badger, giving him a big goodbye hug.

"Come on then, boys, into the car," shouted Mr Rat.

"Race you there!" yelled Reggie Rat, running as fast as his legs would take him.

And with that, they all said their goodbyes, jumped in the car, and waved each other off as Mr Rat drove away, heading for the seaside where they would have lots and lots of adventure.

Of course, Bertie Badger was waving the fastest, and for the longest, he never stopped waving until his arm started aching.

"I can't wait to play on the beach!" said Bertie Badger, smiling.

"I can't wait either!" replied Reggie Rat, *"I think we should build some sand castles when we get there."*

Before they got to the seaside, Reggie Rat and Bertie Badger decided to play a car game.

> Reggie Rat wants to know, if you can guess the name of his favourite game to play in the car?

> Well, his favourite car game is called 'animal in your head' would you like to learn how to play the game?

Bertie Badger had to think of an animal in his head, and then Reggie Rat had to ask up to six questions to try and guess the animal; once he had asked some or all his questions, he also had six guesses to guess what the animal was.

"Okay, Reggie Rat, I'm ready," said Bertie Badger, thinking of an animal in his head.

"Right, no cheating, Bertie Badger!" advised Reggie Rat, being all serious, *"Now let's see, hmm, how many legs does it have?"*

"Four!" giggled Bertie Badger.

"Hmm, what colour is it?" asked Reggie Rat.

"Black and white!" giggled Bertie Badger.

"Hmm, what does it eat?" asked Reggie Rat.

"Grass!" giggled Bertie Badger.

"Okay, I think I know what it is, but I'll ask one more: what noise does it make?" asked Reggie Rat, rubbing his hands together.

"*Moo, moo,*" giggled Bertie Badger.

Thinking for a moment, "*It's a cow!*" shouted Reggie Rat.

"*Well done, my cow impression must have given it away!*" replied Bertie Badger.

After a few more games, they started to play another game. For this game, you had to be the first one to spot a red colour car, then blue, then green, and so on, but they soon became tired and slept for the rest of the way.

Sweet dreams from Reggie Rat

Sunday Night
Reggie Rat at the Seaside

"Wake up, boys, we are here!" shouted Mr Rat.

Reggie Rat and Bertie Badger opened their eyes and looked out the car windows.

> Reggie Rat wants to know, do you remember what games they played in the car?

> Well, it was 'animal in your head' and 'spot the coloured car'.

"We're here, we're here," yelled Reggie Rat, *"Look, Bertie Badger, look at all those dunes."*

"They look awesome; I can't wait to run up and down them," smiled Bertie Badger, putting on his sunglasses to look cool.

Mr Rat pulled up at the beach, paid for the car parking and then drove onto the beach, where he found a lovely spot to park.

The car doors burst open, and Reggie Rat and Bertie Badger excitedly fell out of the car.

"Come on, Bertie Badger; let's go; remember, we're building sand castles!" shouted Reggie Rat, super excited.

"*On my way,*" replied Bertie Badger, hopping on one leg while trying to tug on his wellie boots.

"*No, no, you need flip-flops, not wellie boots for the beach. Have another look in the bag your mum packed,*" suggested Reggie Rat.

"*Roger that!*" replied Bertie Badger, looking through his bag for some flip-flops.

After finding his flip-flops, he slipped them on and checked himself out; then, looking up, he saw the sea for the very, very first time.

"*Wow, the blue sea, it's so beautiful,*" grinned Bertie Badger.

As they sat on their towels admiring the waves for the first time, Mrs Rat came over carrying something that would help protect them from the sun's rays.

> Reggie Rat wants to know, can you guess what Mrs Rat brought over to help protect them from the sun?

> Well, it was a big bottle of sun cream, of course.

"*The sun's rays are very, very hot, and this will help protect you and stop you from burning in the midday sun,*" explained Mrs Rat, handing over the bottle.

"*Okeydokey, Mrs Rat,*" smiled Bertie Badger, slapping on the sun cream everywhere.

Reggie Rat did the same on his legs, arms, face, ears, nose and lastly, his very, very long tail.

All ready and protected, they grabbed their spades and buckets and headed further down the beach to build their sand castles.

"*Right, let's go here; this will make a great place to build our sand castles,*" pointed Reggie Rat, digging the spade into the sand.

"*Okeydokey looks good to me,*" agreed Bertie Badger.

Then, dig, shovel, and pat went the sand; Reggie Rat's sand castle was now beginning to look pretty amazing.

However, Bertie Badger started digging such a big hole that he scooped sand all over Reggie Rat.

"*Stop, stop!*" yelled Reggie Rat, brushing the sand off his towel.

Bertie Badger popped his head out of his hole, and they both giggled as the sand had gone everywhere.

Soon, with Reggie Rat's help, Bertie Badger's sand castle started to look much better with some smoothing out and patting down.

Then, stepping back, they both stood there looking and admiring their magnificent sand castles, dreaming they were knights on horses dressed in shiny armour.

"*I'm hungry, fancy an ice cream?*" asked Bertie Badger.

"*Good idea!*" replied Reggie Rat, licking his lips.

So, off they went to the ice cream van to choose their favourite flavour before returning to their magnificent sand castles.

Licking their melting ice creams, they watched the sea rolling in and out, creeping closer and closer to their sand castles.

> Reggie Rat wants to know, can you guess what the sea will do to the sand castles when it reaches them?

> Well, the sea will make the sand castles disappear, like they were never there.

"*Look!*" yelled Reggie Rat as he watched the waves crashing into their sand castles and knocking down the walls.

"*Well, we had a lot of fun building them,*" said Bertie Badger as he watched them disappear back into the soft yellow sand from where they began.

"*We sure did,*" replied Reggie Rat, "*But best of all, we got to make some cool memories playing at the seaside, especially as this was your first time.*"

By the time they had finished their ice creams, both sand castles stood no more, just waves coming and going.

Sitting on their towels, they talked and giggled while watching crabs sidestep in a rather clumsy yet funny way.

Mr & Mrs Rat pulled up their deck chairs and sat beside them as they watched the sunset in the distance.

Then, all of a sudden, *"Look!"* shouted Reggie Rat, pointing out towards the sea.

Everyone stood up and gazed out toward where Reggie Rat had pointed.

"What's that?" asked Bertie Badger, looking curiously.

"That Young Bertie Badger is a Humpback Whale that lives in the ocean," said Mr Rat, *"And, did you know they can grow to about 60 feet and weigh up to 30,000 tons."*

"Wow, that's incredible," Bertie Badger replied, watching the Humpback Whale spout from his blow hole.

As the sun set on the horizon, they decided it was time to leave, so they all went to find the holiday cottage where they were staying.

Reggie Rat wants to know, can you guess what they did in the car on the way to the holiday cottage?

Well, no car games this time, but they both had another little nap.

While driving, Mr & Mrs Rat smiled as they listened to Reggie Rat and Bertie Badger snoring away in tune with each other.

Sweet dreams from Reggie Rat

A big thank you to...

Reggie Rat

Bertie Badger

Rebecca Rabbit

Harry Hare

Vinnie Vole

Dani Dormouse

Mr Bull

Mr Fox

Mr & Mrs Rat

Bobby Black Bird

Mr Goat

Benjamin Buzzard

Mr & Mrs Badger

Readers & Listeners

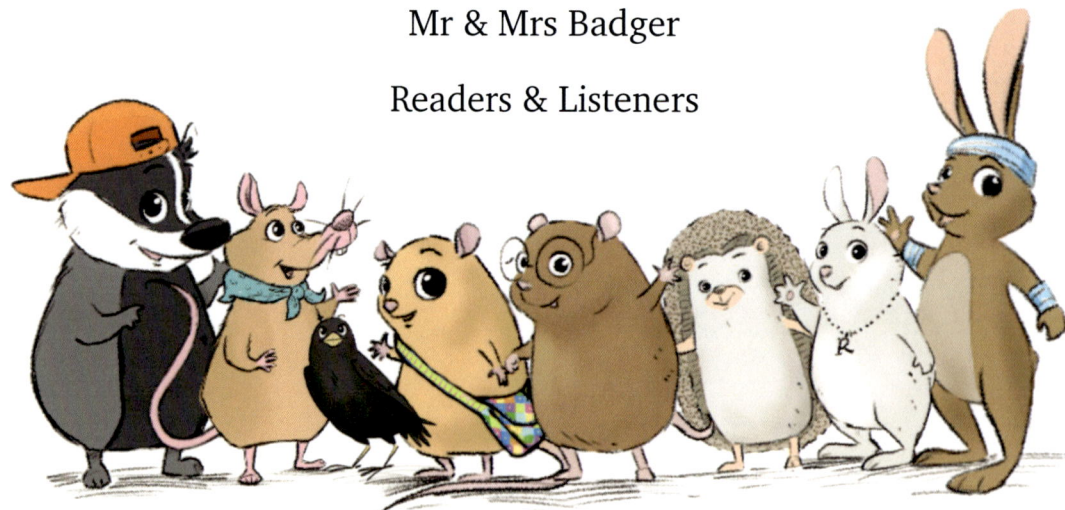

Other Books Available

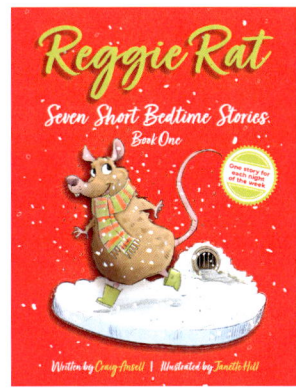 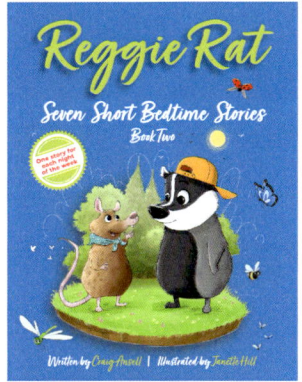 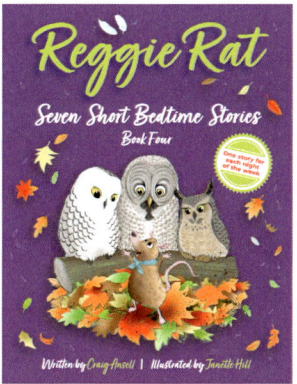

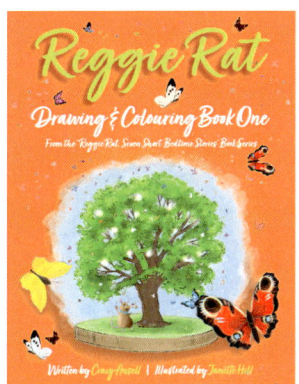 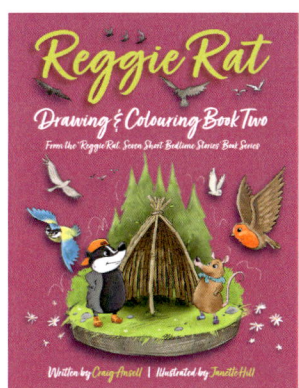 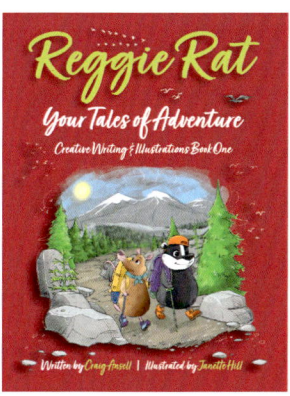

Look out for more books coming soon...

Follow us
 Reggie Rat and Friends

Available from
reggieratandfriends.com

Feedback & Reviews

Reggie Rat would love to hear your feedback; which story was your favourite? Did you like the illustrations? Did you enjoy the Q & As. Well, now that you're part of Reggie Rat's family of friends, why not write a review on whichever site you made the purchase?

www.ingramcontent.com/pod-product-compliance
Lightning Source LLC
Chambersburg PA
CBRC090902080526
44587CB00008B/177